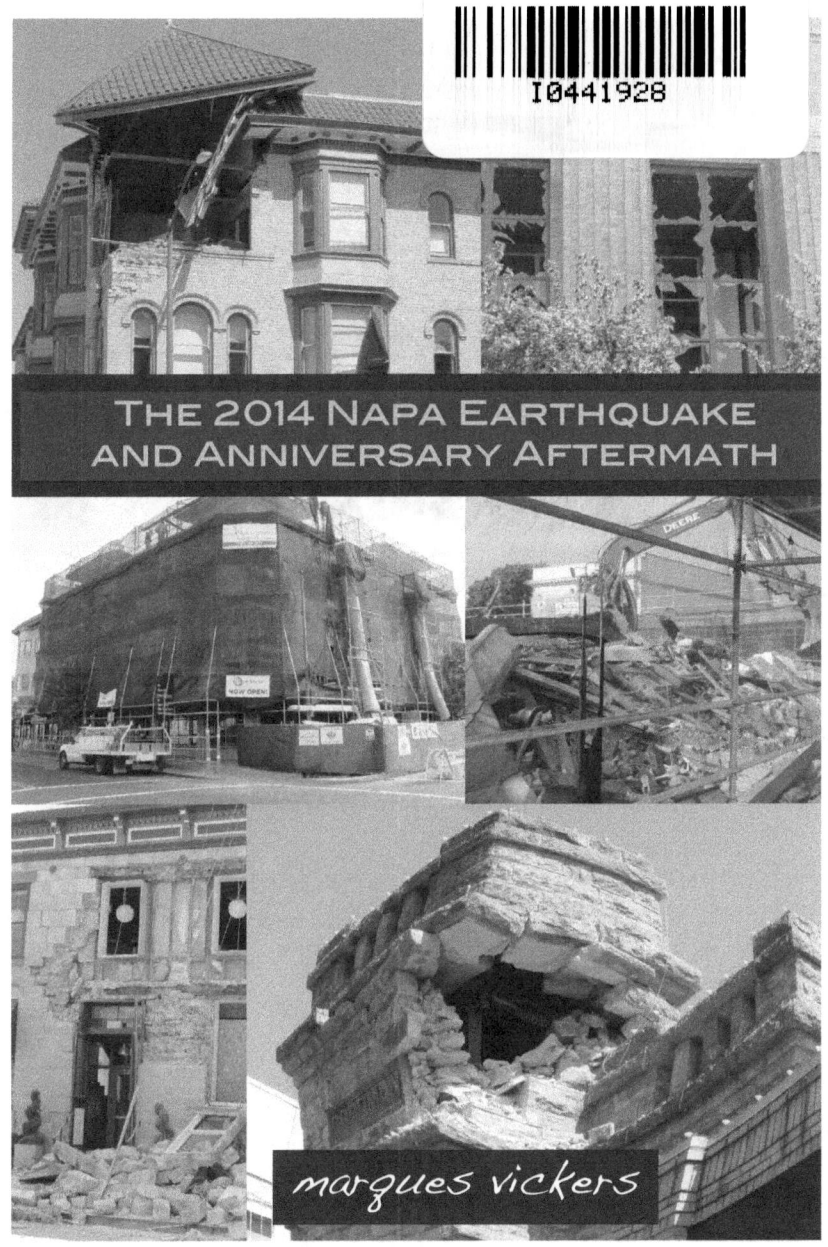

The 2014 Napa Earthquake
and Anniversary Aftermath

marques vickers

The 2014 Napa Earthquake and Annivesary Aftermatch
A Fourteenth Month Retrospective Into Historical Downtown Napa

Marques Vickers

**MARQUIS PUBLISHING
CONCORD, CALIFORNIA**

Version 1.1

Published by Marquis Publishing
Part of Marquis Enterprises
Concord, California USA

Vickers, Marques, 1957

The 2014 Napa Earthquake and Annivesary Aftermatch: *A Fourteenth Month Retrospective Into Historical Downtown Napa*

To Those Awakened at 3:20 A.M. To Realize Their World Had Abruptly Been Altered. To My Daughters Charline and Caroline.

Table of Contents

Preface

About the Author

Preface

When a 6.0 magnitude earthquake awakened me at 3:20 a.m. from the dead of sleep, the event is memorable. Immediately afterwards, my cell phone lit up providing, at this hour, the only illumination. Calls concerned with my safety poured in from all over the globe. The realization hit…I was near the epicenter.

On Sunday morning, August 24, 2014, the lash of a whip rudely awakened the Napa Valley region. This sensation was the effect of a five-second-earthquake jolt. Another ten to fifteen seconds of shaking followed decreasing in intensity.

The experience was dreamlike. Living at the time in nearby Vallejo, I felt a sense of paralysis amidst the darkness. In the midst of an earthquake, one speculates when or if the rattling and movement will end. There is no question – control belongs to nature.

What followed depended upon your proximity to the epicenter. If you were nearby, free standing and mounted objects often followed the forces of gravity falling to the floor. The shattering noise of ceramics and glass was often deafening. Then silence. The pause was unnerving since traditionally worse aftershocks often followed.

In a bewildered daze, Napa residents surveyed the debris and many joined their neighbors in the darkened streets.

This mere twenty seconds had altered their existence.

The Napa Valley had never experienced a direct earthquake hit of this magnitude. The oasis of Victorian-era buildings nestled amongst vineyard laced hillsides seemed somehow immune from the legacies of other damaged communities that had suffered from the shifting of the San Andreas faultline. Nature, however, has an extended memory. The unreinforced masonry of nineteenth and early twentieth century constructions had always been seismically vulnerable. The alluring Victorians failed this test. Their quaint charm proved defenseless against errantly vibrating terrain.

Many downtown residents fled the insecurity of their homes in the dark and wandered throughout the historic quarter. Immense chunks of rubble and broken glass littered the streets. Napa's architectural heritage staggered prone. A county courthouse, post office, two century old churches, the Sam Kee Laundry, Goodman Library and the worst, the Alexandria Annex were now fractured and exposed. Gaping holes left building facades and roofing open to the elements. Damage and debris were strewn indiscriminately, seemingly everywhere.

The temblor was centered six miles south of Napa in the city of American Canyon a buffering town of 20,000, adjacent to Vallejo. It was the largest earthquake to victimize the San Francisco Bay Area since the magnitude 6.9 Loma Prieta quake struck in 1989. The Loma Prieta earthquake collapsed part of the Bay Bridge roadway and killed more than 60 people, most when a section of Oakland freeway collapsed.

The geography around the American Canyon epicenter consisted predominantly of soft muds, helping reduce the scope and scale of the damage by reducing shaking at the ground level.

The quake ruptured 60 water main and gas lines. Electricity for over 30,000 customers was immediately severed. The local hospitals treated approximately 200 emergency room patients, most suffering from lacerations, bruises and broken bones. Throughout Napa, there was evidence of collapsed walls, chimneys, carports and even a few buckled asphalt roads. There were six reported fires, the most prominent at a mobile home park where four units were destroyed and two damaged. A ruptured water main delayed firefighters efforts to fight the blaze, reminiscent of the water system failings of the infamous San Francisco quake and fire of 1906.

While Napa suffered the worst of the damage, there was also significant impairment about 17 miles south in downtown Vallejo and Mare Island, a former naval shipyard. Thirteen Victorian officer's mansions on Walnut Street suffered diverse internal and external damage. Each shared the fate of detached chimneys littering their front lawns due to unreinforced masonry. Severed water mains caused significant flooding to the U.S. Forest Service and Touro University building complexes located on the southwest sector of Mare Island.

Many downtown Vallejo commercial buildings suffered moderate damage with broken plate glass along Tennessee Street and several red and yellow-tagged structures on Georgia Street. Red-tagged buildings were deemed unsafe. Yellow-tagged indicated that owners would be going in only to clean the premises. Public operations would not be permitted until city officials authorized each building's safety.

The most prominent casualty within downtown Vallejo was the First Baptist Church located on the corner of Sonoma Boulevard and Carolina Street. The church was red-tagged and deemed unfit for occupation due to the fear the bell tower had been structurally weakened to the point it might collapse. Built in the 1920's, the church had been retrofitted in the 1990's. The earthquake had cracked and splintered sections of the old tower. On August 26th, the tower was dismantled piece by piece to insure the safety and survival of the structure.

This building bore personal significance. It was the church where my parents were married in and my sisters and I attended and spent our formative years.

The morning and afternoon of Sunday, August 25th were calm. Clean up commenced and nearly all of the downtown Vallejo and Napa businesses remained shuttered. Monday morning, normal activity resumed. The media were wrapping up their reportages as the novelty and public interest had subsided. The Napa wine harvest, originally scheduled for Monday evening was delayed slightly. Timing however is critical in wine production and any delay influences the complexity and quality of the harvest.

Northern Californians are adaptive to catastrophe and nature's excess. Earthquakes are the tariff exacted for choosing a desirable and superior lifestyle. Since that fateful Sunday morning at 3:20 a.m., there have been approximately 60 aftershocks, the strongest reported at magnitude-3.6.

The true aftershocks have arrived amidst the rehabilitation of downtown Napa and for the owners of approximately 200 homes and buildings in various states of disrepair and habitability. Suffering, hope and ultimately reconstruction has created a succession of narratives illuminating human resiliency and our capacity to rebuild and endure despite tragedy.

The accompanying media circus covering the quake has long ago uprooted their reflector tents and cameras. Restoration lacks dramatic intensity. Coverage is conspicuously absent from front-page headline news.

The current stages of repair and renovation are a slow arduous process often lacking immediate visual evidence. Developers, financiers, building and business owners, government officials and residents have coped with the inconveniences and inefficiencies that a natural disaster imposes. Yet over one year later, the visual victories from repairs begin to become apparent and a cohesive refurbishment evident.

My forth edition documents the one-year anniversary of the restoration. I have made periodic visits to downtown Napa beginning the day following the quake and during October 2014 and January, May and November 2015. The comparative photographs showcase the progression of repair and the fusion of a downtown core being regenerated. The cost has not come cheap. An estimated $500 million has already been spent with the expenses far from complete.

Over 200 photographs visual chronicle the change and the heroic efforts of downtown revitalization, focusing on historical buildings of local significance. The collective efforts continue and with the construction of the Napa Center project centering the core, there is significant reason for continued optimism.

Alexandria Hotel

The most media photographed casualty on the day following the earthquake was the landmark Alexandria Hotel and Annex Building on the corner of Second and Brown Streets. The Alexandria was also known as the Plaza Hotel. Built in 1910, the hotel was the design of architect William H. Corlett and his design exemplified the Mission Revival and Mediterranean Revival styles, both popular in California during the early twentieth century.

Later in his career Corlett would design the Depression era Franklin Street Main Post Office. The Alexandria design featured three-square towers on the street facing corners, overhanging eaves, and slanted bay and rounded windows.

During the seismic turbulence, the walls on the supporting top floors crumbled showering extensive brick and mortar onto the sidewalk. The building's brick walls were bolted from floor to ceiling but still exposed the greatest vulnerability of unreinforced masonry. Weak mortar joints between bricks crumbled enabling chunks of stones and bricks to adhere to the laws of gravity.

The disintegrating walls could not support the weight of the decorative towers and each leaned and teetered precariously at an angle towards the street below. The towers however did not fall and within two months were removed and lowered down to Brown Street.

Extensive renovation work on the Alexandria was initially delayed due to the potential damage hazards. By early 2015, the towers had been relocated into storage and the building scaffolded and protectively wrapped. Over the subsequent months, masonry and fractured drywall boards have been lowered into refuse bins and renovation work has been extensively completed within the inside core.

The corner towers have been reattached and integrated into the design. During my final November 2015 photo session, the building remained wrapped but completion is nearing. When the wrapping will be finally removed, the Alexandria will display its former architectural luster and a page of tragic Napa history will have turned.

October 2014

October 2014

October 2014

January 2015

January 2015

May 2015

May 2015

November 2015

November 2015

Franklin Station Main Post Office

The Franklin Station post office was the city's oldest and primary postal center. The post office was built in 1933 with funding from the Federal Public Works Administration. Architect William H. Corlett, who also designed the Alexandria Hotel Annex, was responsible for the Art Deco styled edifice. The front facade of the structure has three sections. The central has six bay windows divided by piers with terra cotta capitals. A terra cotta cornice is adorned with ram and cow's heads resting atop.

The side sections, which contain the building's two entrances, feature panels with decorative eagle designs above the doorways and urn-shaped bronze light fixtures on each side. The post office's lobby showcases a painted bas-relief plastic ceiling, unusual in federally constructed post offices, and a terrazzo floor.

The significant structural damage, asbestos presence in the interior and exorbitant renovation estimates has proven beyond the financial capabilities of government relief efforts. A conclusion that the building would require demolition drew immediate criticism from historical preservation societies and local residents.

There are no simplistic solutions based on the extent of the damage.

The building remains frozen, portraying the original damage suffered from the earthquake. Masonry and foundation cracks remain evident. The shattered windows remain boarded up on the facade and steel support braces remain installed on the damaged corners and shifted columns of brick. The front corner urns and decorative lights have been wrapped and the building remains enclosed by a protective chain link fence.

The strangest irony is that damage appears minimal to the rear and both sides of the structure. The large plate windows are intact and their glass was never broken.

After withdrawing the demolition option, the building was put up for sale. Any purchaser would have to adhere to very stringent renovation standards. Whether the building is even structurally repairable for public occupancy is the primary concern.

Until this dilemma is resolved, the Franklin Post office remains the single most contrary repair from the devastating quake.

October 2014

October 2014

October 2014

January 2015

January 2015

January 2015

January 2015

May 2015

May 2015

November 2015

November 2015

November 2015

The Sam Kee Laundry
The Sam Kee Laundry, also known as the Pfeiffer Building is located at the corner of Main and Clinton Streets. It was constructed in 1875 and is Napa's oldest stone and commercial building. The Pfeiffer began as the Barth Brewery until 1890 when it became the Stone Saloon, complete with accommodating brothel in the upper floor.

In the 1920s, it became the Sam Kee Laundry and acquired its current identity. Sam Kee contributed to Chinese-American history with his victory in a landmark court case. He successfully challenged the constitutionality of a city ordinance created in 1887 that made it illegal to have a laundry operating within city limits. The ordinance was clearly discriminatory against Chinese-Americans since they predominately managed laundry operations during the era.

From 1976 to 1999, the building housed the Andrews Meat Company and Deli. In 2002, it became the Vintner's Collective, a tasting and sales outlet for 18 local wineries without their own tasting rooms. The building features a simple stone facade design topped by a decorative Italianate cornice.

Although the earthquake damaged the facade extensively, the building was one of the fastest and most aggressively renovated. Much of the facade masonry and windows from the northeast quadrant of the building, including the entire lower level window, fell to the street below exposing the wood framing and insulation.

The Vintner's Collective operated throughout the reconstruction, re-routing their entrance through the rear. Today, the façade stones have been painstakingly refitted back into place and the structure resembles its pre-earthquake appearance.

October 2014

January 2015

January 2015

January 2015

January 2015

May 2015

May 2015

November 2015

November 2015

November 2015

First Methodist Church

The impairments to the First United Methodist Church located at Fifth and Randolph Streets originally appeared fatal. The most prominent damage consisted of a sanctuary wall drifting away from the building. The wall of the church constructed in 1917 was in danger of eminent collapse.

The structure traced its origins back to an elemental brick edifice constructed on the identical site in 1867. That building was razed to accommodate the current sanctuary building nearly a century ago.

While undergoing reconstruction, services were relocated to the Napa Community Seventh-Day Adventist Church. The church offices isolated from the sanctuary remained fully operational.

The errant sanctuary wall was braced back into position. The cracking and detail fracturing was meticulously repaired. A fresh coat of paint has made the transformation seemingly miraculous.

October 2014

October 2014

January 2015

January 2015

January 2015

May 2015

May 2015

May 2015

November 2015

November 2015

November 2015

Winship-Smernes Building

The Winship-Smernes Building located at the corner of Main and First Street suffered minimal damage, primarily from shattered storefront plate glass windows and superficial surface cracking and loss on the wall facing the parking lot of the building.

The building was constructed in 1888 and designed by a locally favored architect Luther Turto who was also responsible for the Goodman Library. The style is typical of late 19th Century commercial architecture, a two-story Italiante Victorian with a cast iron and glass storefront. The original tower was removed following the 1906 San Francisco earthquake. A turreted tower was reinstalled in 1985 during an extensive renovation and restoration.

The scaffolding used to resurface the damaged wall was removed by the end of 2014 following a reported $100,000 in repairs. The building was repainted and accented with gold gilted highlights. The principle lower level tenant is currently the Napa Valley Coffee Roasting Company.

October 2014

October 2014

October 2014

January 2015

January 2015

May 2015

May 2015

November 2015

Napa County Courthouse

The historic Napa County Superior Court building was constructed between 1878-79 and designed by the Newsom Brothers, California's foremost Victorian architects of the era. Constructed with local masonry, the structure was an example of the High Victorian Italiante style. It originally featured an Octagonal bell tower, which was damaged during the 1906 San Francisco Earthquake and removed in 1931 out of public safety concerns.

The most prominent homicide case tried in Napa's history was that of film pioneer Eadweard Muybridge for the murder of Harry Larkin during a jealous rage in a Calistoga mining camp in 1874. Muybridge's stroboscopic continuous image sequences were a direct precedent to motion pictures.

The trial was held in the building, which preceded the construction of the present facility. Muybridge had discovered that Larkyn had fathered a child he believed was his son. Muybridge's attorney pleaded an insanity defense for his client. Despite Muybridge's admission of premeditation, the jury acquitted him finding the killing *justifiable*. The verdict became another example of the influential advantages of celebrity.

Napa's Courthouse lawn has the dubious distinction of hosting the last public execution by hanging within California in 1897.

The most visible damage to the courthouse structure was an enormous gaping hole in the northwest corner of the facade and evident roof detachment. The building remains wrapped for precautions against the elements with 9000 square feet of low-density polyethylene plastic. The current plastic replaced an earlier tarp that proved too flexible and prone to swaying and falling with wind gusts. Steel braces stabilized by concrete pillars have been installed to fortify the center facade.

Since the earthquake reparations have begun, partial operations have returned in the later constructed additions to the courthouse (1910s and 1930s). These offices include Family Court Services, Jury Assembly and Court Administration.

October 2014

October 2014

October 2014

January 2015

January 2015

January 2015

May 2015

May 2015

May 2015

November 2015

First Presbyterian Church

The First Presbyterian Church constructed in 1874 in the Neo-Gothic style is located at the corner of Third and Randolph Streets. Bricks were dislodged around the bell tower and the bell tumbled off its perch. Two chimneys collapsed and a balcony stairway was loosened. Five principle panels from the large stained-glass window on the facade collapsed. The quake sent glass and bricks showering to the steps in front and left piles of broken plaster inside. The weather vane on the church's steeple tilted erratically noting the catastrophic tenor of events.

The stained glass panels remain boarded up and protected by mounted plastic due to the required reparation funding and delicate nature of their repair.

The weather vane atop the steeple remains crooked.

January 2015

January 2015

May 2015

November 2015

Napa Law Center and Adjoining York Building Complex
The Napa Law Center building located on Brown Street was prominently photographed following the earthquake for the collapse of a portion of its southern wall on an unfortunately parked car in an adjoining parking lot. The detached southern wall section teetered precariously for a few weeks following the quake until propped and shored back into position by specializing machinery. The ill-fated automobile was presumably scrapped. The building, constructed in 1904 appears to be in the process of having damaged stonework on its front facade repaired and reinforced.

The adjacent York Building complex is composed of two buildings with significant local history. Constructed in the 1870s in conjunction with the County Courthouse, the structure has formerly served as the Napa City Hall, City Council Chambers, Jail and Police Department offices. A north facing wall of the building was reinforced during the same time as the southern wall section of the Napa Law Center. The adjacent York Building ultimately was demolished.

October 2014

October 2014

October 2014

October 2014

October 2014

January 2015

January 2015

January 2015

May 2015

May 2015

November 2015

November 2015

Goodman Library Building

The Goodman Library Building located on 1219 First Street suffered significant structural damage and most visibly a gaping hole and loosening of stones in the fortress styled crown adorning the top of the building. Built in 1901, the library was paid for by George E. Goodman and built on land donated by Goodman. Architect Luther M. Turton designed the building in the Richardson Romanesque style, which can be seen in its use of rusticated stone, round arch windows, and massive scale. The design represented a shift in Napa architecture, which was mainly Victorian prior to the library's construction.

The Goodman Library is the longest-operating library in California, partially due to a clause in Goodman's donation of the building. Goodman stipulated that the building would remain in the city's possession as long as it served as a library but would otherwise revert to his heirs. When Napa moved its city library to a different building in the 1970s, the Napa County Historical Society acquired the building for its research library so it would still satisfy its original purpose. The library now houses both the Historical Society and Napa County Landmarks.

The library book collection was reportedly salvaged with minimal damage following the earthquake and securely stored until the museum ultimately reopens.

Due to the financing intricacies involved for reimbursement through Federal Emergency Management Agencies, renovation was initially delayed. Repairs are currently underway.

The building remains surrounded by scaffolding and protective mesh. A completion date has not been announced.

October 2014

January 2015

January 2015

May 2015

November 2015

November 2015

Coles Chop House, Grand Hand Gallery, Wine Country Group Real Estate and TORC Restaurant

Work began the day after the earthquake to refit and reinforce the stone masonry on the Main Street facade hosting the TORC Restaurant, Grand Hand Gallery, Wine Country Group Real Estate and Cole's Chop House. The refurbishment was promptly completed and the building returned to full operation.

October 2014

October 2014

January 2015

January 2015

May 2015

November 2015

Napa Andaz Hotel

Napa's Andaz Hotel opened in 2009 as an Avia brand hotel on the corner of First Street and Franklin. In the world of real estate speculation and exchange, it has been a frequently traded pawn. In 2011, it was part of a Hyatt Hotel acquisition from Avia's parent company Lodgeworks and in 2012, the Avia was renamed the Andaz Napa. After being listed in the Spring of 2013 by Hyatt, the property was purchased by Inland American Real Estate Trust of Oak Brook, Illinois. Hyatt continues to manage the property described an upscale boutique concept hotel.

The building sustained surface facade damage from the earthquake which has since been refinished.

January 2015

November 2015

Napa Firefighters Museum

Not every structure in the historic downtown district has arrived at a conclusive ending. The Napa Firefighters Museum building on the corner of Pearl and Main Streets was closed permanently. The reasons were due to a combination of earthquake damage and desire by the city to sell the building since 2012 when California dissolved all community Redevelopment Agencies.

The Museum was established in 1996 and displayed a variety of historic firefighting engines and equipment. The existing contents and displays are in the process of being redistributed into diverse other locations or put into storage.

A panel of the south wall fell onto the Pearl Street sidewalk and resulting gap remains boarded up. The building also suffered from ceiling cracks and loosened window attachments.

Currently, a broken glass pane near the front entrance has been replaced, but the plywood concealing the fallen wall remains boarded. Antique fire remains housed inside.

A definitive decision on restoration or resale has not been determined. Given its prime location and proximity across the street from the future Napa Center development, demand for the property should be high and demolition a probable option.

May 2015

November 2015

Coombs to Clinton Street Pedestrian Bridge
The downtown pedestrian Coombs to Clinton Street Bridge has been closed since the earthquake due to ankle bolts at the bottom of the bridge being sheered off. The bridge was originally installed in late 2007. The renovation and refurbishment process has begun, but the bridge remains closed.

May 2015

November 2015

November 2015

Napa Center Development Project

The transformation of the downtown Napa business core was ironically fast forwarded by the August 24th earthquake. Initially the damage created a significant confidence challenge to a previously proposed outdoor mixed-use retail, office and accommodation project.

The ambitious Napa Center development originally comprised over 130,000 square feet of retail space centered by a five-story, 183-room flagship hotel, the Archer Napa. The Archer would face a block of First Street stretched between Main and Coombs Streets.

The Napa Center is intended to include two and a half blocks of frontage space along First Street and a contemporary mix of entertainment, cultural venues and wine tasting showcases. Existing commercial properties will be absorbed into the project as well as over 40 new retailers and restaurants. The overall land parcel for the development encompasses the boundaries of Pearl Street (northern), First Street (southern), Franklin Street (eastern) and Main Street (western).

Once renovation and refurbishment work accelerated within the downtown center, the ambitious and extent of the project have expanded as well. The total potential retail square footage has increased to 380,000 square feet due to property acquisitions including the most prominent existing Kohl's Department Store.

Most importantly, tangible evidence is visible that construction is not simply a developer and city planner's blueprint fantasy. Demolition of the Archer Hotel site has been completed and construction is underway. As the rebar and concrete layers elevate vertically, the realization that transformation will occur becomes evident to the skeptics and detractors.

There have been many of both. The Archer Hotel construction was delayed an entire year, not due to the earthquake, but because a grievance filed by a North and East Bay Area Hotel Union group requiring public hearings. The union's multiple claims consisted primarily of "insufficient preservation efforts by the developers". The union group lost on both their initial claim and appeal but effectively escalated legal expenses and time delay. Curiously, the union reportedly did not represent a single worker in any existing Napa hotel. Their intentions and motivations stirred up significant local debate.

Large-scale ambitious municipal retail developments like the Napa Center are volatile creations. Over the years, downtown Napa has been propositioned with a variety of failed projects that usually neglected to materialize due to the lack of financing and firm tenant commitments.

The Napa Center presently appears tangible and substantive. Extensive renovation work on several prominent buildings is in process. The former Sushi Mambo Building, once appearing hopelessly crippled, has been resuscitated into a jewel. Smaller retail intended buildings along the Franklin, Randolph and Coombs alleys have been polished and soon will be readied for tenancy. The upgrades have been complimented by attractive walkways, innovative public art installations, seating areas, landscaping and integrated fountains.

Developer Todd Zapolski has been steadfast from inception regarding his vision and design of a shopping complex that reflects *a modern agrarian feel that is authentic to Napa*. The intricate pieces and reformation have begun to fit into place. This evolution arrives in stark contrast to a downtown that has previously lacked cohesion and definition.

The Gordon Building on First Street currently awaits its refurbishment, surrounded by fencing. The Dunne Building has been stripped solely to its ornate mosaic tilted façade. The framing structure is undergoing structural reinforcement and preparation to become integrated into the Archer Hotel complex. The former Toscana restaurant property was razed in November 2015. Modernized structures will begin to fill in the spacing gaps until integration is complete.

There are numerous elements towards proper fusion that require time, patience and imagination to fully visualize the end result. As the evidence mounts, the cynics will have less to criticize and instead a credible and vibrant downtown to utilize and appreciate.

Time will ultimately judge the credibility and vision of the Napa Center project. The initial progress has been exemplary.

First National Bank Building
Encapsulated within the Napa Center project, but owned independently, the First National Bank building has staged many commercial roles during its history including banking, retail, community group meeting hall and presently the Restorante Allegra. The Classical Revival style building suffered damage to one of the cornice pillars along with other superficial facade wear. Damaged holes and pitting have been patched and grouting reinforced to create a finished appearance for a longtime community landmark.

October 2014

October 2014

October 2014

October 2014

October 2014

October 2014

October 2014

October 2014

October 2014

October 2014

January 2015

January 2015

January 2015

January 2015

January 2015

January 2015

January 2015

January 2015

January 2015

January 2015

January 2015

January 2015

January 2015

January 2015

January 2015

January 2015

January 2015

May 2015

May 2015

May 2015

May 2015

May 2015

May 2015

May 2015

May 2015

May 2015

May 2015

May 2015

May 2015

November 2015

November 2015

November 2015

November 2015

November 2015

November 2015

November 2015

November 2015

November 2015

November 70's

November 2015

Visual Artist, Writer and Photographer Marques Vickers re-
established his northern California art and creative operations
following a five-year residence in southern France between
2005-2009. His figurative painting, photography and sculptural
works have been sold and exhibited internationally since 1986
(MarquesV.com).

Born in 1957, Vickers grew up in Vallejo, California. He is a
1979 Business Administration graduate from Azusa Pacific
University in the Los Angeles area. Following graduation, he
became the Executive Director of the Burbank, California
Chamber of Commerce between 1979-84. He later served as Vice
President of Sales for AsTRA Tours and Travel in Westwood,
California between 1984-86.

Following a brief residence in Dijon, France, he founded
Marquis Enterprises in 1987. His operations included sports
apparel exporting, fine wine brokering and travel and tour
operations until 2005 with his relocation to the southern France
region of the Languedoc.

Returning from his French residence in 2009, he began the
Marquis Gallery (ArtsInAmerica.com) focused on reselling rare

books, collectibles, fine art and wine through online marketplace stores and barter exchanges. Vickers has written extensively on the fine arts, auction industries, southern France and various photojournalism projects. His distribution company Marquis Publishing, sells his electronic and paperback books through numerous online bookseller outlets.

He has two daughters, Charline and Caroline, both residing in France.

BOOKS:
Marketing and Buying Fine Art Online, Allworth Press, New York NY (2005)
Making Auction Pay, Marquis Publications, Vallejo CA. (2014)
Unicorns and Dark Chocolate: Eros, Aphrodesia and Existence, Marquis Publications, Vallejo CA (2014)
Amour, Wine and Real Estate, Marquis Publications, Vallejo CA (2014)
Flamenco Jondo: The Paintings of Marques Vickers, Marquis Publications, Vallejo CA (2014)
The Ultimate Guide to Selling Art Online, Marquis Publications, Vallejo CA (2014)
The Lafayette White Cross Memorial, Marquis Publications, Vallejo CA (2014)
2014 Napa Valley Earthquake, Marquis Publications, Vallejo CA (2014)
Fish Head Beach: The Silent and Senseless Murders of Lindsay Cutshall and Jason Allen, Marquis Publications, Vallejo CA (2014)
Muse One: Pantera Linda, Marquis Publications, Vallejo CA (2014)
Nature As Art: One, Marquis Publications, Vallejo CA (2014)
Springtime in New England, Marquis Publications, Vallejo CA (2014)
San Antonio Riverwalk, Marquis Publications, Vallejo CA (2014)

Ruined Castles and Phantom Memories, Marquis Publications, Vallejo CA (2014)

Sand and Water: Desert and Seascapes, Marquis Publications, Vallejo CA (2014)

Napa Rebuilds: Two Months Following Their Devastating Earthquake, Marquis Publications, Vallejo CA (2014)

The 2014 Napa Valley Wine Harvest, Marquis Publications, Vallejo CA (2014)

The Topography of Evil: Notorious Northern California Murder Sites, Marquis Publications, Vallejo CA (2015)

The Disappearing Women, Marquis Publications, Morro Beach CA (2015)

Five Month of Renovation After the 2014 Napa Earthquake, Marquis Publications, Morro Bay CA (2015)

100 Famous Phobias and Obsessions: An Entertaining Portrayal of Anxiety, Fears and Insecurity As Artwork, Marquis Publications, Morro Bay CA (2015)

Visions of Neo-Urbania: The Reinvention of Contemporary Metropolitan Vertical Living and Commerce, Marquis Publications, Tacoma WA (2015)

Nature As Art Two: Photography and Abstract Paintings of Marques Vickers, Marquis Publications, Tacoma WA (2015)

Morro Rock: Veiled Bridge of the Nine Sisters, Marquis Publications, Tacoma WA (2015)

Eternal Spring Street: Los Angeles' Architectural Reincarnation, Marquis Publications, Tacoma WA (2015)

The Reflective Powers of Water As Visual Alchemy, Marquis Publications, Tacoma WA (2015)

Jimi Hendrix, Bruce and Brandon Lee and the Lakeview Cemetery Seattle: Entombing Our Icons, Marquis Publications, Renton WA (2015)

The Artistic Properties of Reflective Glass, Marquis Publications, Renton WA (2015)

The Glass Curtain Architecture of Bellevue, Washington, Marquis Publications, Renton WA (2015)

Murder in California: Notorious California Murder Sites,
Marquis Publications, Renton WA (2015)
*Coffee Anarchists of the World Unite: The Italian Roasted Elixirs
of Tacoma, Washington*, Marquis Publications, Renton WA
(2015)
*The Abandoned Western Cascade Mountain Railroad Tunnels
and 1910 Wellington Avalanche*, Marquis Publications, Renton
WA (2015)

www.ingramcontent.com/pod-product-compliance
Lightning Source LLC
Chambersburg PA
CBHW072200280526
45788CB00002B/816